RECORDED VERSIONS GUITAR

AUTHENTIC TRANSCRIPTIONS
WITH NOTES AND TABLATURE

LYNYRD SKYNYRD

Transcribed By PATRICK MABRY

ISBN 0-7935-3533-6

W9-BYN-624

COVER PHOTO BY JEFFREY MAYER

Additional Transcribers: "Free Bird" & "Sweet Home Alabama", Andy Aledort;
"What's Your Name", Chris Amelar; "Gimme Three Steps", Jeff Perrin.

HAL•LEONARD
CORPORATION

7777 W. BLUEMOUND RD. P.O. BOX 13819 MILWAUKEE, WI 53213

The Ballad of Curtis Loew

Words and Music by Allen Collins and Ronnie Van Zant

white cur - ly hair. _____ When he had a _ fifth of wine, _____ he did not have a care. _____
and may - be I was ten. _____ Ma - ma used to whoop me _ but I'd go see him a - gain. _____
bod - y came to pray. _ Old preach-er said some words and they chunked him in the clay.

He used to own an old do - bro, _ used to play it cross _ his knees. _____ I give old _ Curt my mon - ey he'd
I'd clap my hands, stomp my feets, try to stay in time. _____ He'd play me a song or two then
Well he lived a life - time play-in' the black man's _ blues. _ And on the day he _ lost his life that's

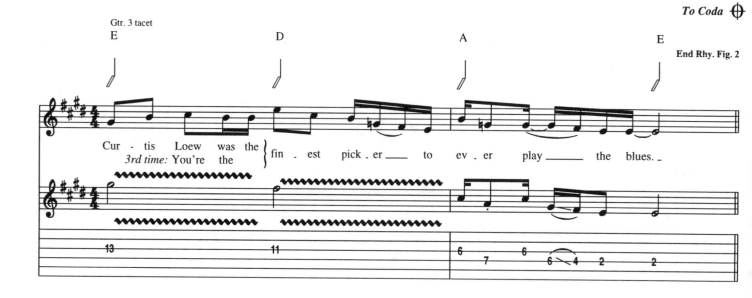

Gtr. 3 tacet

End Rhy. Fig. 2

Cur - tis Loew was the { fin - est pick - er —— to ev - er play —— the blues. —

3rd time: You're the

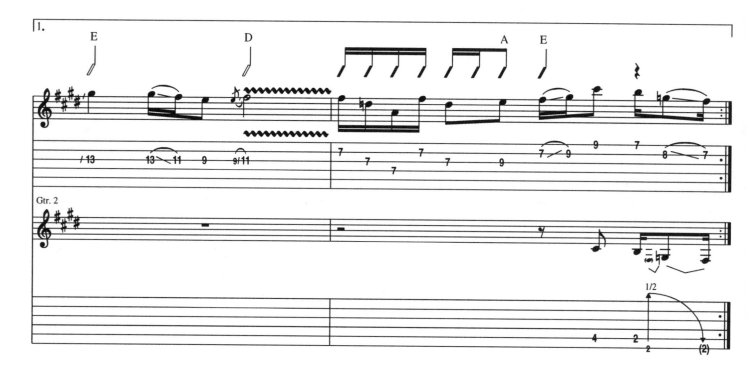

1.

Gtr. 2

1/2

2.

Gtrs. 2, 3 & 4

Gtrs. 3 & 4

Gtr. 2 cont. in notation

Gtr. 2

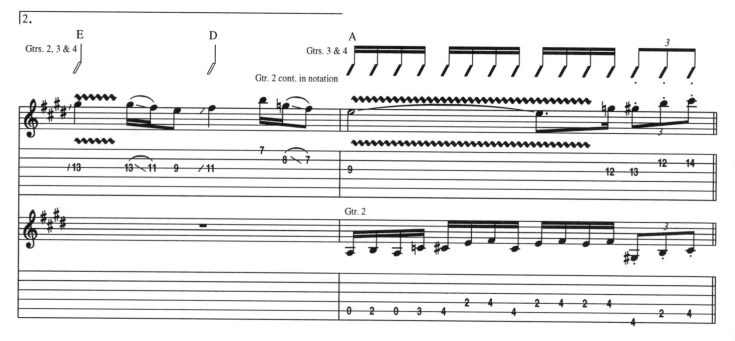

Guitar Solo

Gtrs. 2, 3 & 4: w/ Rhy. Figs. 1 & 1A, 2 times

Gtr. 1 tacet
Gtrs. 2 & 4: w/ Rhy. Fig. 2
Gtr. 3: w/ Rhy. Fill 1

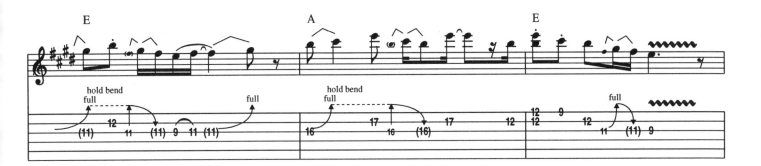

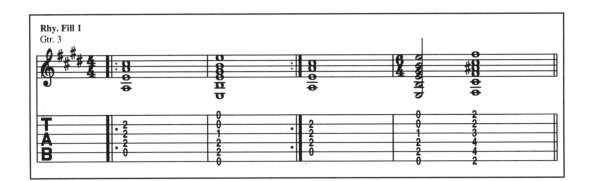

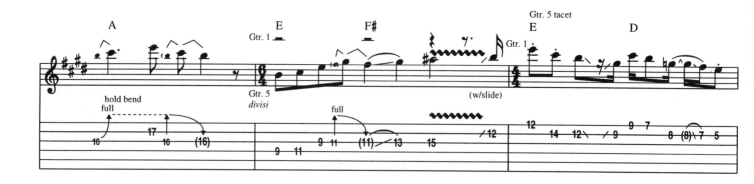

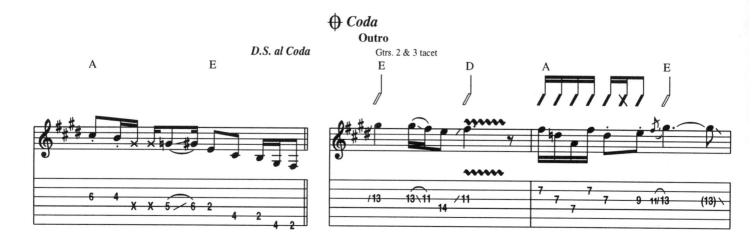

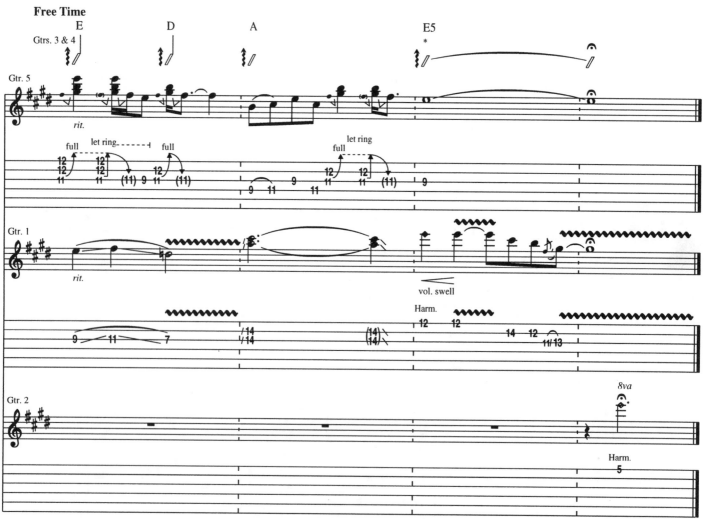

Don't Ask Me No Questions

Words and Music by Ronnie Van Zant and Gary Rossington

MCA music publishing

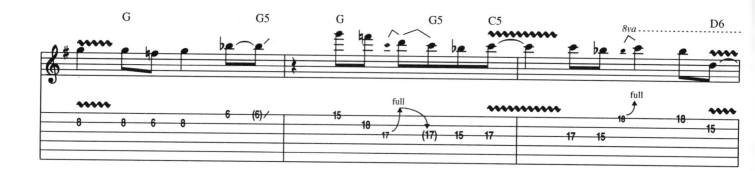

D.S. al Coda
(take 2nd ending)

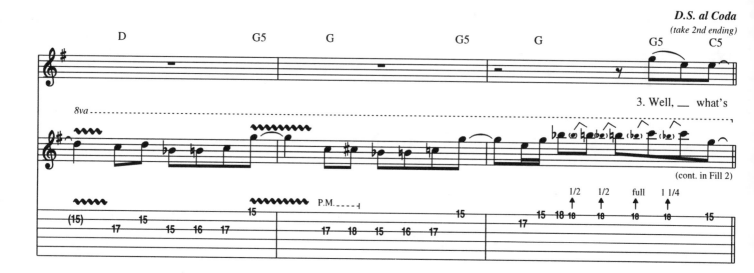

3. Well, ___ what's

(cont. in Fill 2)

Coda

Gtr. 1: w/ Rhy. Fig. 1

Gtr. 2: w/ Fill 4

___ I ___ said don't ask ___ no stu-pid ques - tions, and I won't ___ send a you ___ a - way.

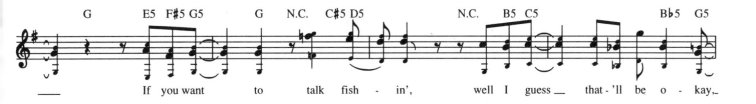

If you want to talk fish - in', well I guess __ that - 'll be o - kay,_

Outro

Gtr. 1: w/ Rhy. Fig. 2, 1st 2 meas. only

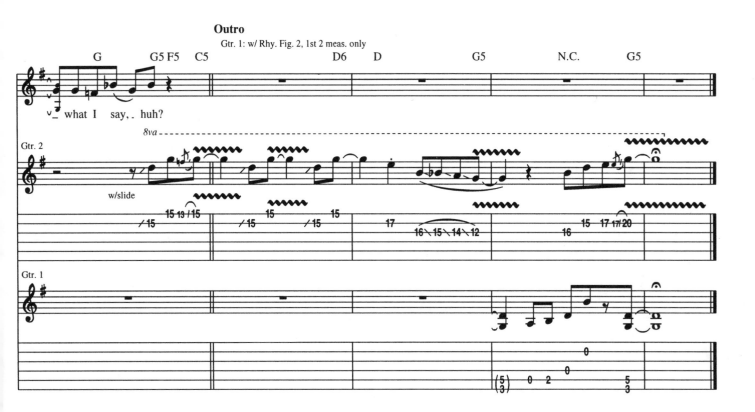

what I say,_ huh?

Additional Lyrics

3. "What's your fav'rite color and
   Do you dig the brother," it's drivin' me up the wall.
   And ev'ry time I think I can sleep
   Some fool has got to call.
   Well, don't you think that when I come home
   I just wanna little peace of mind?
   If you wanna talk about the bus'ness,
   Buddy you're just wastin' time. *(Chorus)*

Down South Jukin'

Words and Music by Ronnie Van Zant and Gary Rossington

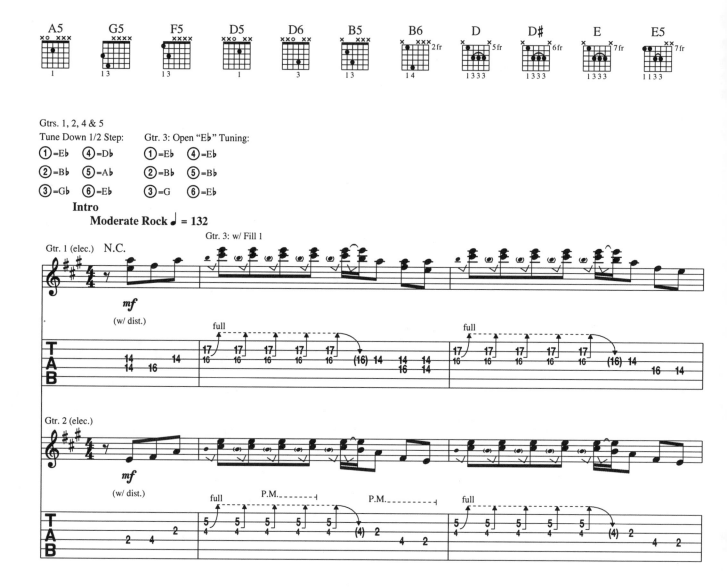

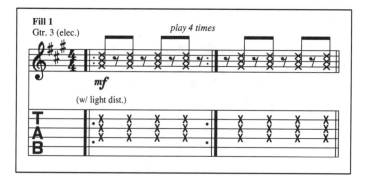

MCA music publishing

place all se-cured, got the ice-box full of wine. _____
work-in' all week and I think ___ it's time we let go. _____
do-in' our thing for pop-pin' all the beer. _____

He said, "A
He got a
We'll o-ver -

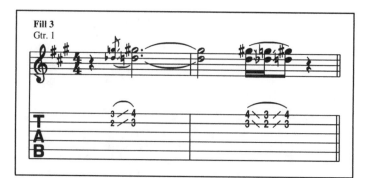

hur - ry on o - ver an' don't be late." He got three love-ly la-dies who just won't wait. Do some
three fat ma-ma's sit - tin' all a - lone. Gon-na sip our wine, Lord, get it on. And do some
come Fri-day night when we head to town, try-in' to pick up an - y wom-an hang-in' a - round. Do some

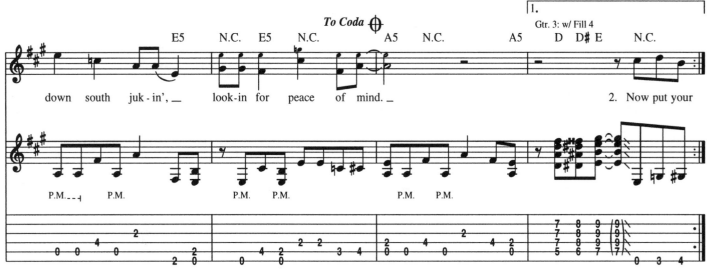

down south juk - in', look-in for peace of mind.

2. Now put your

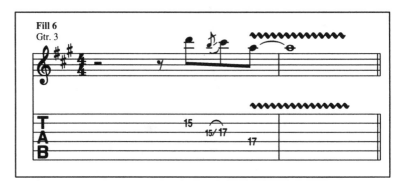

Fill 6
Gtr. 3

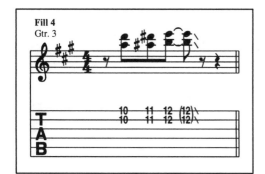

Fill 4
Gtr. 3

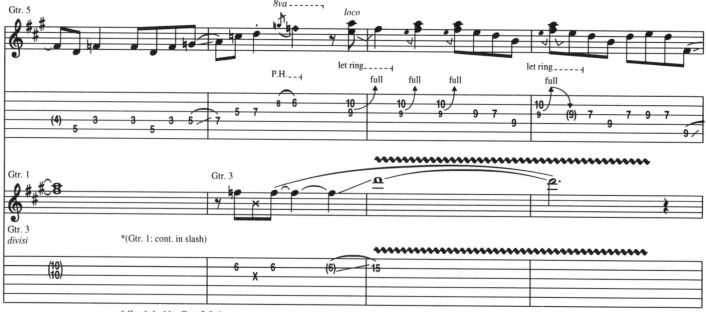

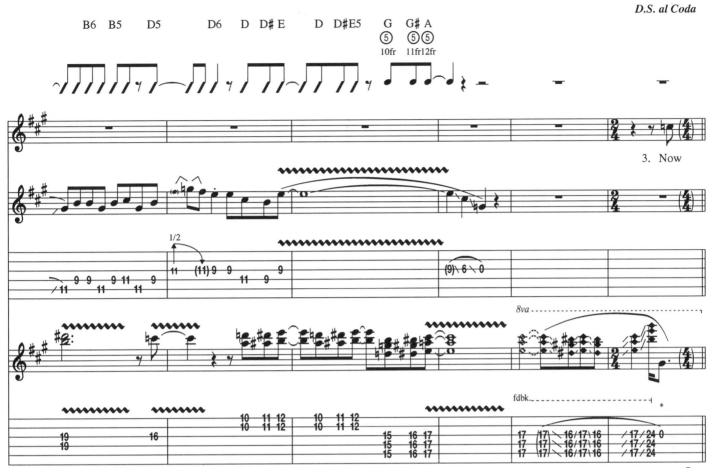

* Slide up off neck sounds open ③ stg.

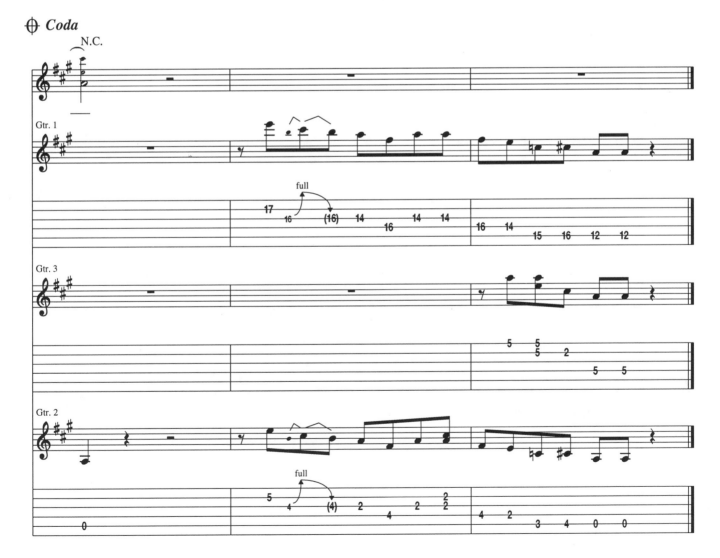

Free Bird

Words and Music by Allen Collins and Ronnie Van Zant

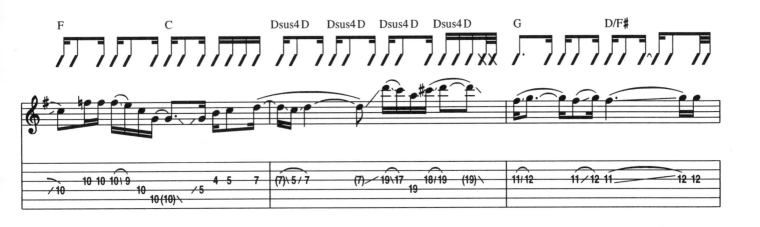

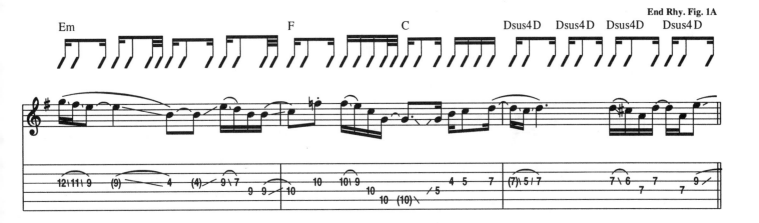

End Rhy. Fig. 1A

Verse

Gtr. 1: w/ Rhy. Fig. 1A, 2 times
Gtr. 2: w/ Rhy. Fig. 1, 4 times

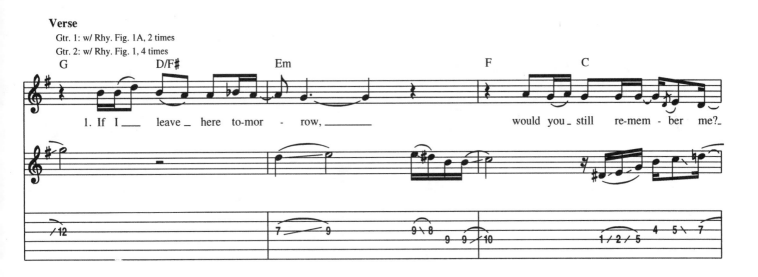

1. If I ___ leave ___ here to-mor - row, _____ would you ___ still re-mem - ber me?_

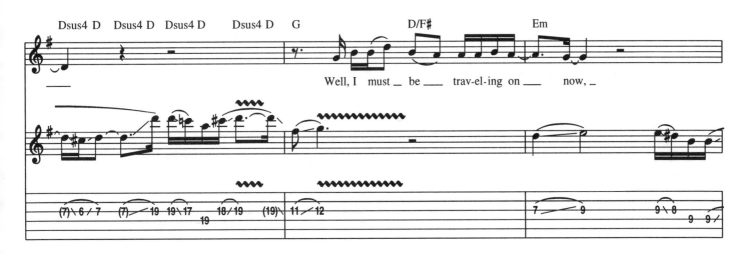

Well, I must ___ be ___ trav-el-ing on ___ now, _

'cause there's too man-y plac - es I've got to see. ___ But if I ___ stay ___ here with you,

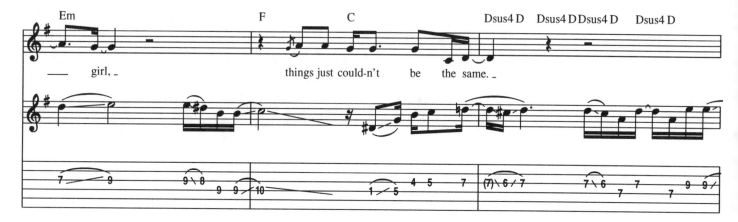

___ girl, __ things just could-n't be the same. __

'Cause I'm as __ free __ as a bird __ now, __ and this bird __ you can-not change. __

_____ Oh, _____ and the bird __ you can-not change, ____

22

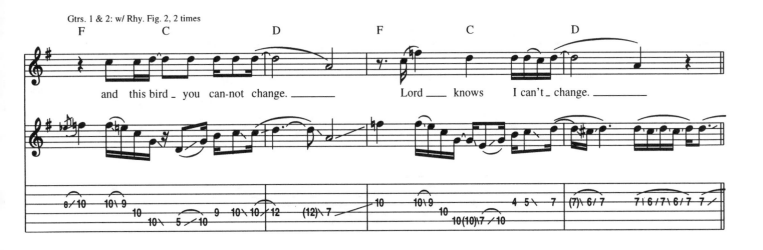

and this bird _ you can-not change. _____ Lord _ knows I can't _ change. _____

Interlude
Gtr. 1: w/ Rhy. Fig. 1A
Gtr. 2: w/ Rhy. Fig. 1, 2 times

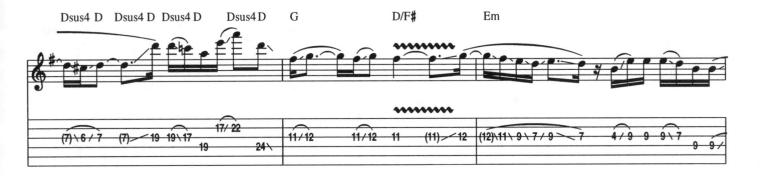

Verse
Gtr. 1: w/ Rhy. Fig. 1A, 2 times
Gtr. 2: w/ Rhy. Fig. 1, 4 times

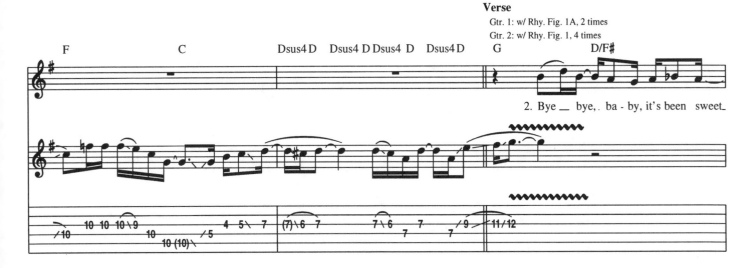

2. Bye _ bye, _ ba - by, it's been sweet_

now, ___ yeah ___ yeah. ___   Though this- feel - in' I ___ can't_ change. ___

A please don't _ take ___ it so _ bad - ly, ___   'cause the Lord knows I'm to blame. ___

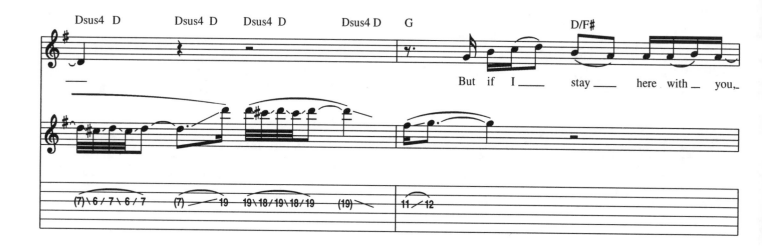

But if I ___ stay ___ here with _ you,_

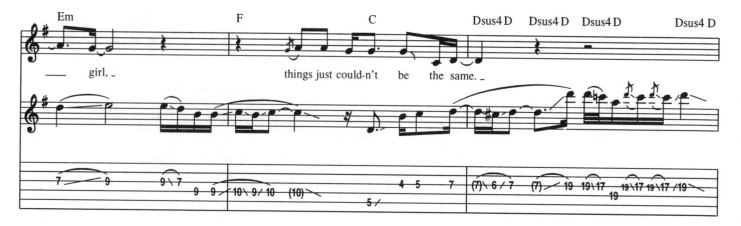

___ girl, _   things just could-n't be the same. ___

Lord, _____ I can't __ change. _____ Won't you

fly, _____ free _____ bird, ___ yeah! _____

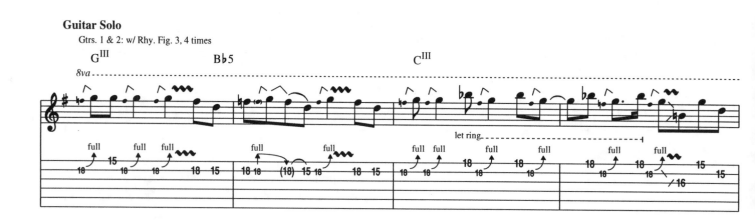

Guitar Solo

Gtrs. 1 & 2: w/ Rhy. Fig. 3, 4 times

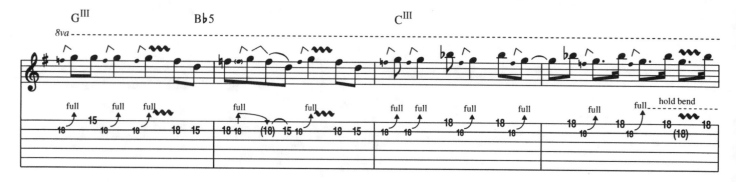

*Rhy. Fill 2 replaces last meas. of
Rhy. Fig. 5 each time

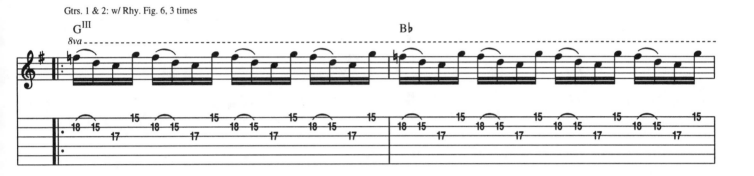

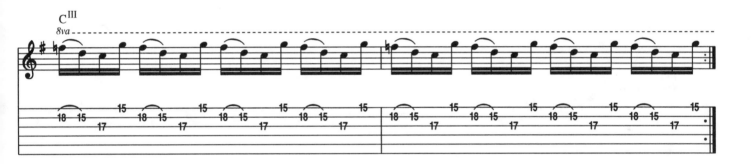

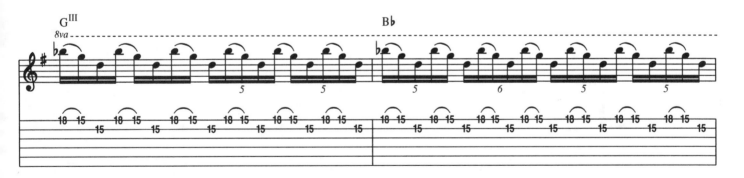

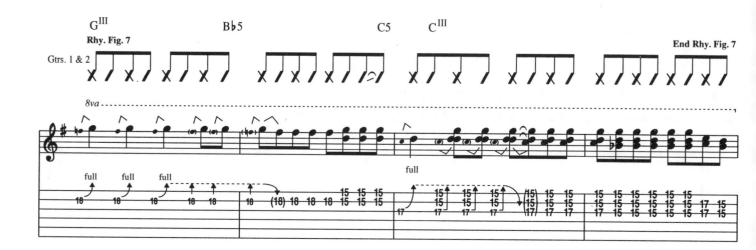

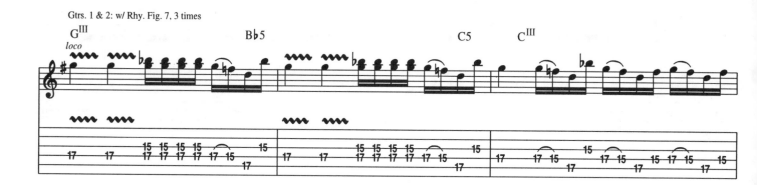

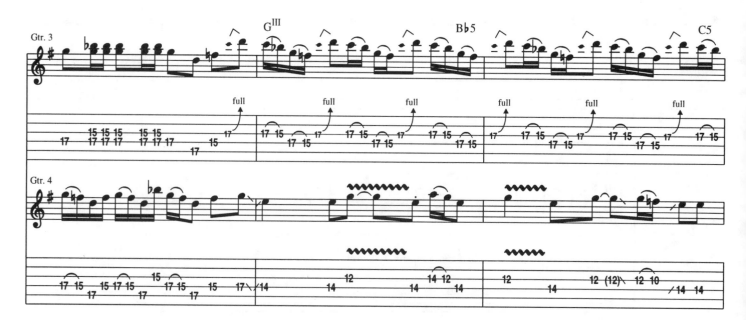

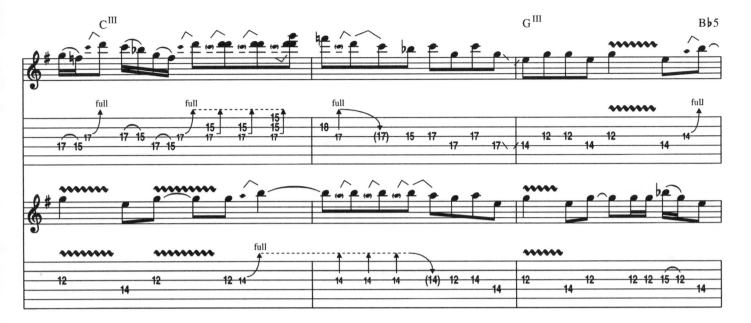

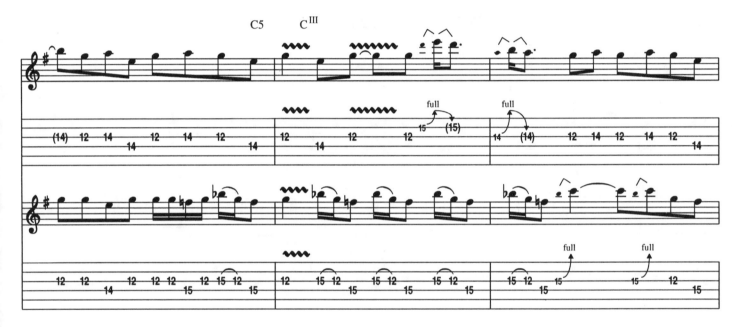

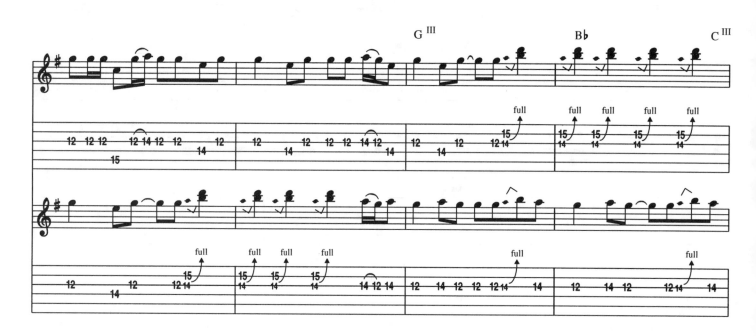

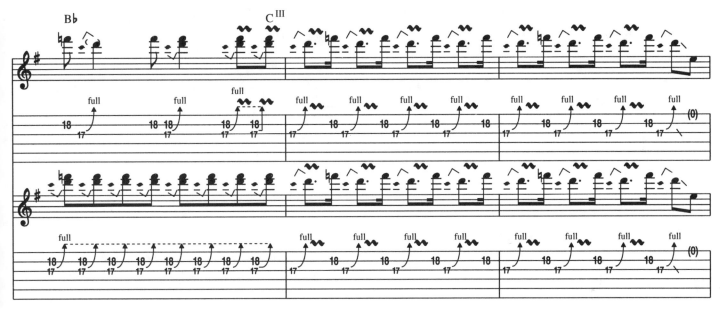

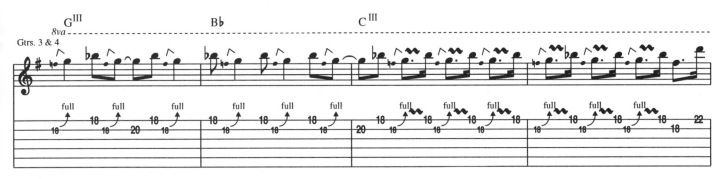

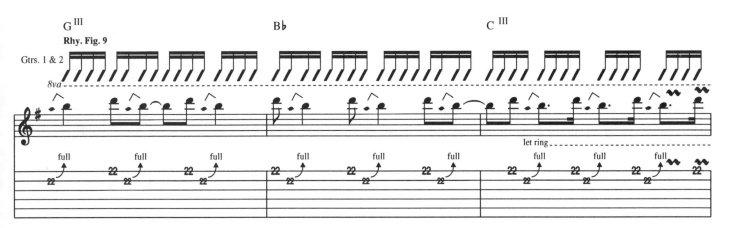

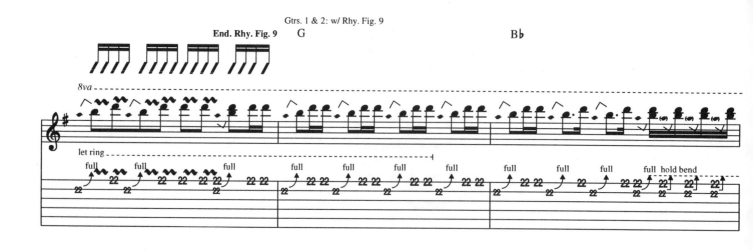

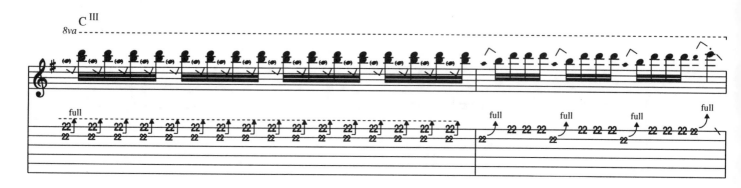

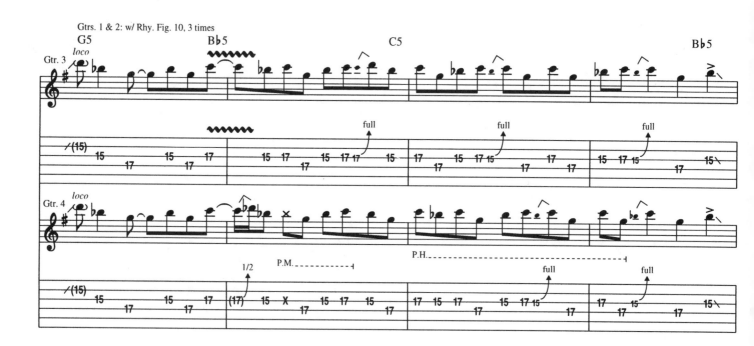

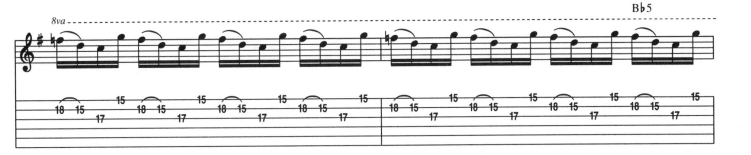

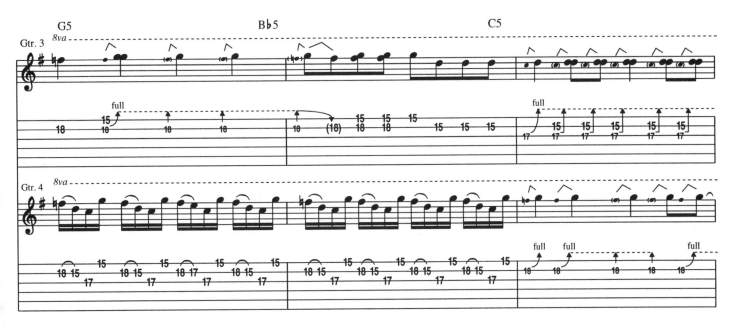

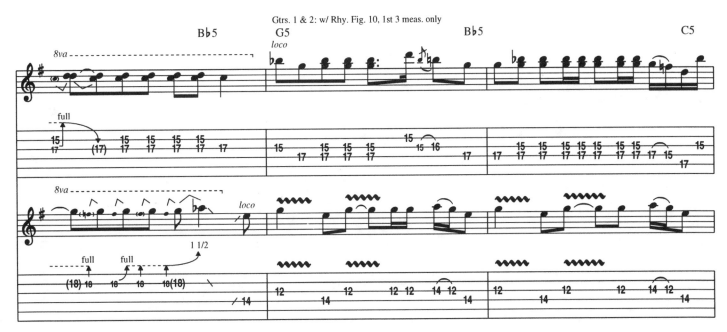

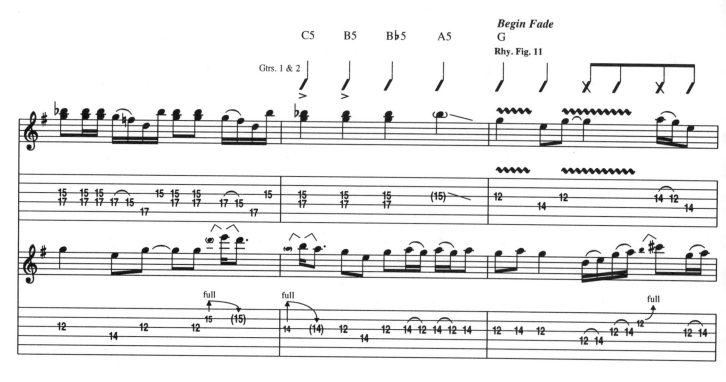

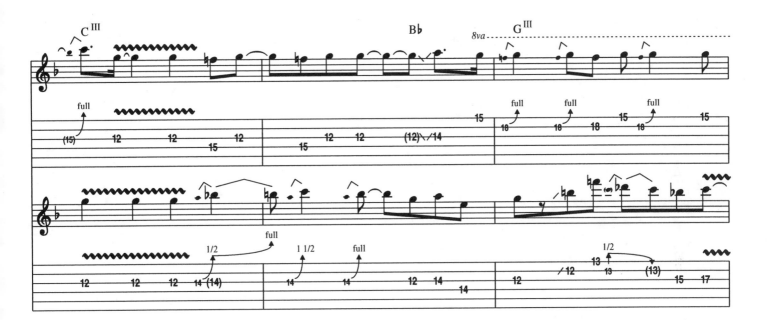

Gimme Back My Bullets

Words and Music by Gary Rossington and Ronnie Van Zant

All Gtrs. Tune Down 1/2 Step:
①= Eb ④= Db
②= Bb ⑤= Ab
③= Gb ⑥= Eb

MCA music publishing

Verse

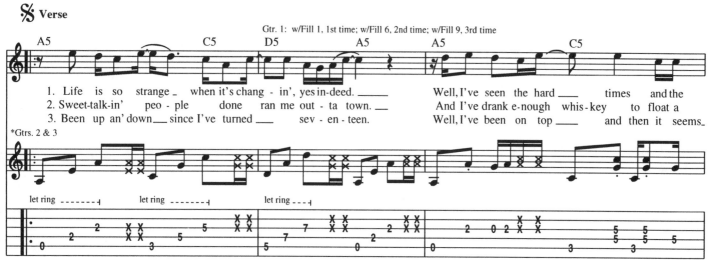

Gtr. 1: w/Fill 1, 1st time; w/Fill 6, 2nd time; w/Fill 9, 3rd time

1. Life is so strange when it's chang-in', yes in-deed. Well, I've seen the hard times and the
2. Sweet-talk-in' peo-ple done ran me out-ta town. And I've drank e-nough whis-key to float a
3. Been up an' down since I've turned sev-en-teen. Well, I've been on top and then it seems

*Gtrs. 2 & 3

let ring

* 2 gtrs. arr. for 1.

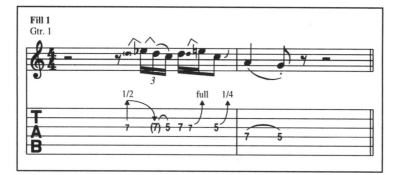

Fill 1
Gtr. 1

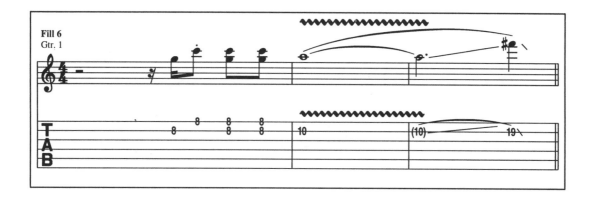

Fill 6
Gtr. 1

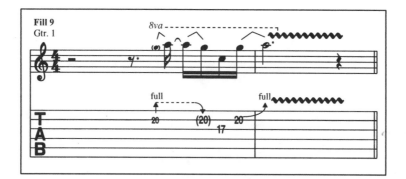

Fill 9
Gtr. 1

pres-sure has been on me. _____
bat - tle - ship a - round. _____
____ I lost the dream. _____

But I keep on a work-in' like a work-in' man do. _____
But I'm leavin' this game one ___ step ___ a-head a' you. _____
But I've got it back, ___ I'm feel-in' bet - ter ev' - ry day. _____

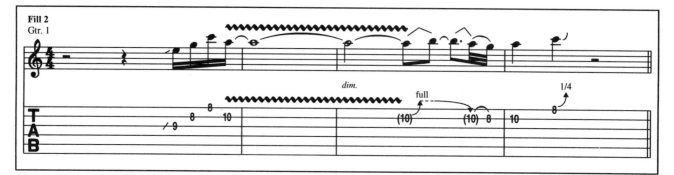

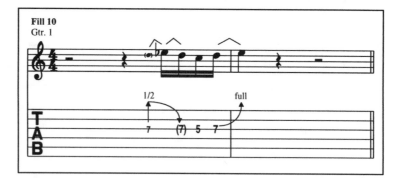

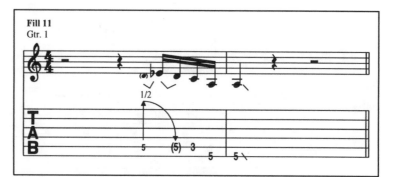

And I've got my _ act to-geth - er, gon-na walk all o - ver you. } Gim-me back my bul - lets.
And you will not _ hear me cry, _ 'cause I do not sing the blues.
Tell all those pen - cil push - ers bet - ter get out-ta my way.

Gtr. 1: w/Fill 4

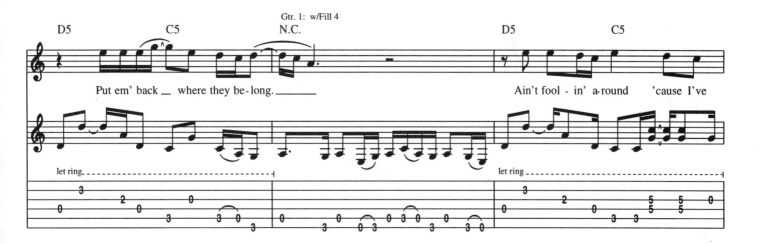

Put em' back _ where they be-long. _____ Ain't fool - in' a-round 'cause I've

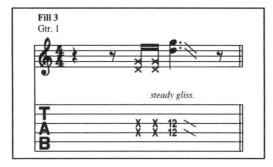

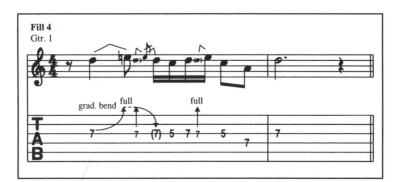

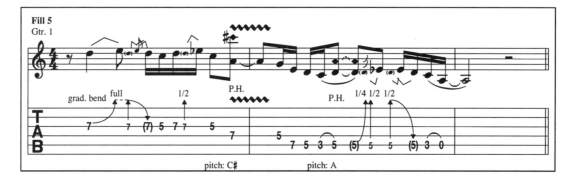

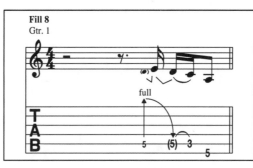

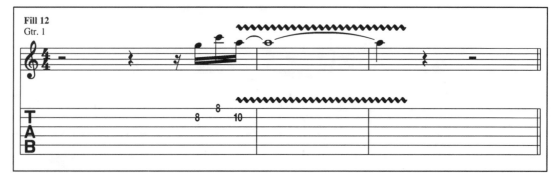

We'll get a - long. _

Guitar Solo

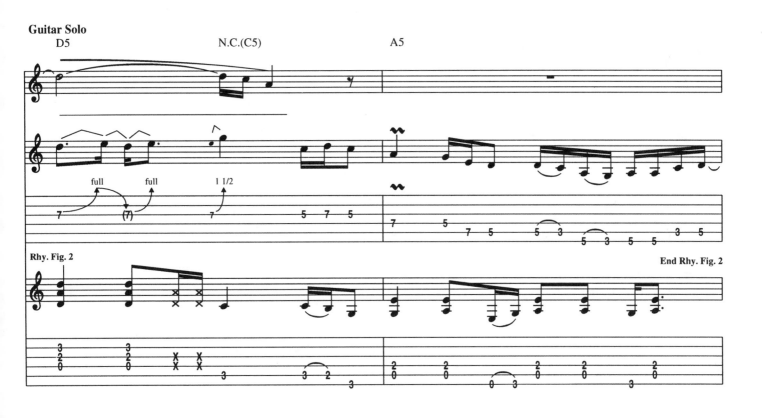

Gtrs. 2 & 3: w/Rhy. Fig. 2, 2 1/2 times simile

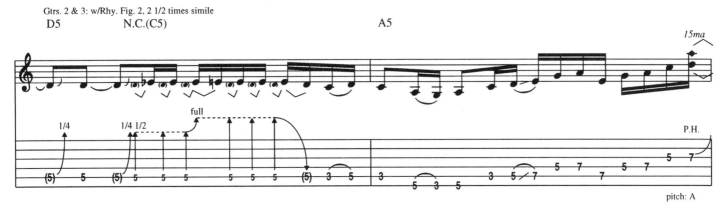

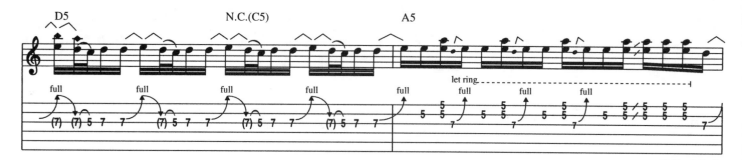

D.S. al Coda

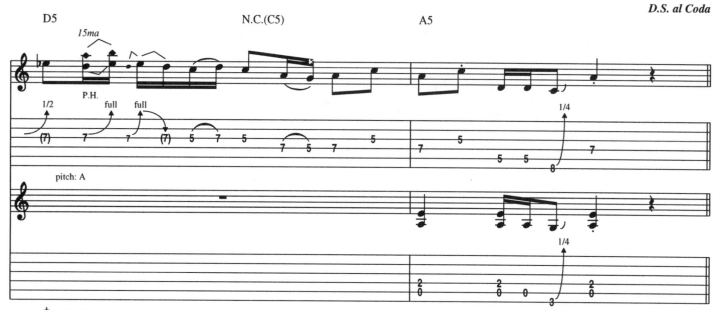

Coda

more dam-age done. Gim-me back, Gim-me back my bul-lets. ___

Gimme Three Steps

Words and Music by Allen Collins and Ronnie Van Zant

MCA music publishing

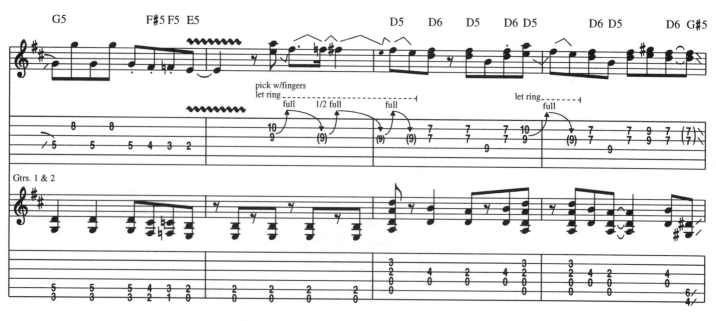

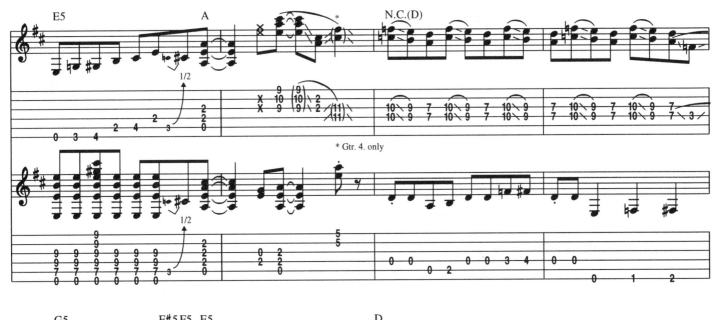

* Gtr. 4. only

D.S. al Coda
(take 2nd ending)

3. Well, the

⊕ *Coda*

Outro Guitar Solo

Gts. 1 & 2: w/ Rhy. Fig. 1, 2 times

Gtr. 3

Spoken: Show me your back door.

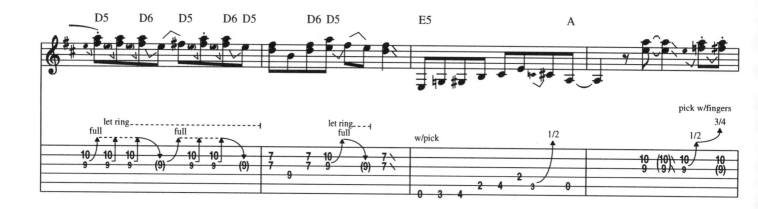

Begin Fade

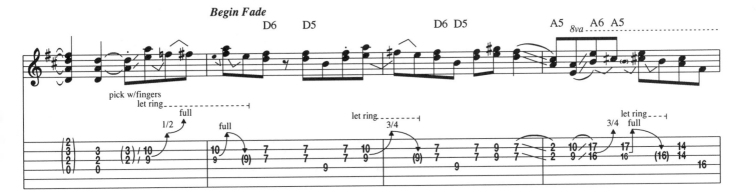

Gtr. 1: w/Rhy. Fill 8

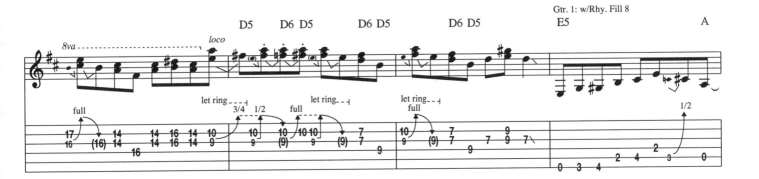

Fade Out

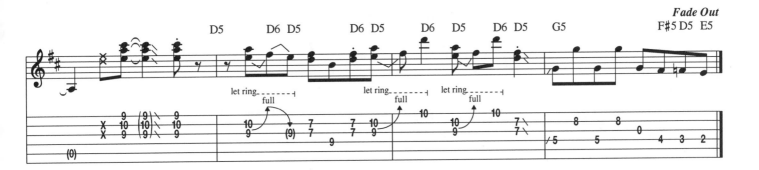

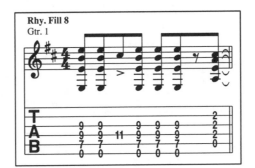

I Ain't The One

Words and Music by Allen Collins and Ronnie Van Zant

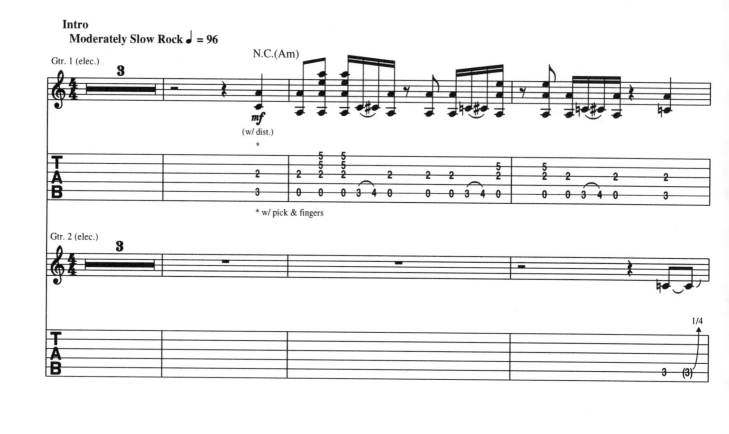

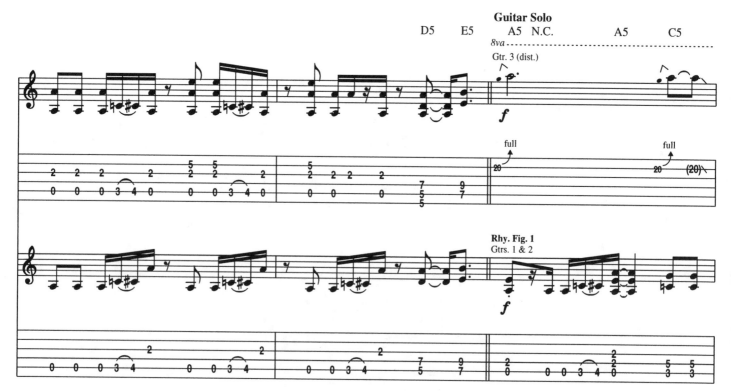

MCA music publishing

Verse

Gtr. 3: w/ Fill 1, 1st time; w/ Fill 2, 2nd time

1. Now I'll tell ya plain - ly, ba - by,   what I plan to do. _   Say I may be cra - zy, wom-an,
   you talk - in' ____ jive, _ wom - an,   when you say to me _   that your dad - dy's gon' take us in, ba - by,

Gtrs. 1 & 2

but I ain't no fool. _   So your dad-dy's rich, ma - ma,   you're o - ver-due. _
take _ care o' me. _   You know and I know, wom-an,   I ain't the ___ one. _

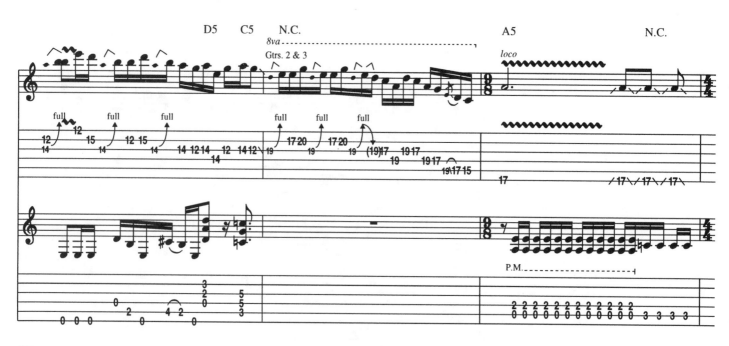

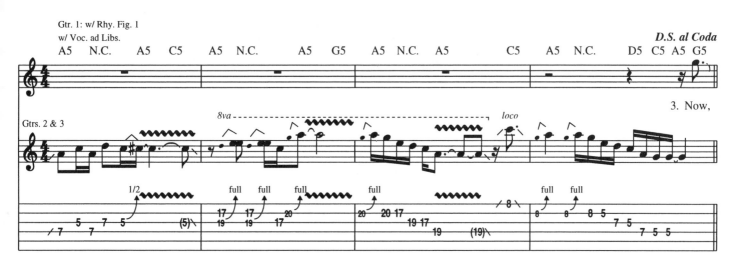

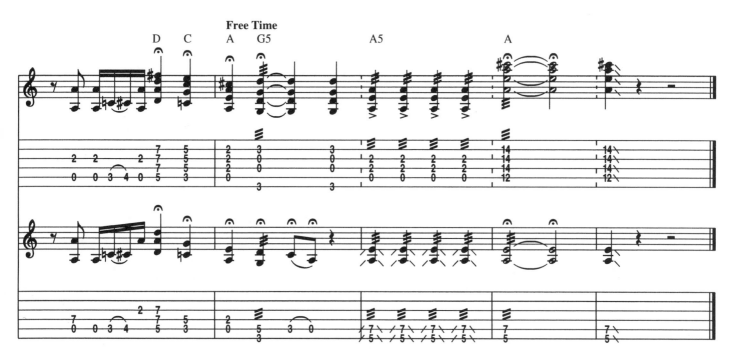

The Needle and the Spoon

Words and Music by Allen Collins and Ronnie Van Zant

MCA music publishing

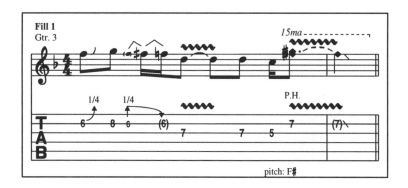

pitch: F#

Chorus

"Tell me son, _ why do ya stand there cry'n?" _ It was
"You bet - ter quit_son be - fore you're dead," _ With the nee - dle _ and the spoon, _
You'll have your chance to hear this some - day. Don't mess with

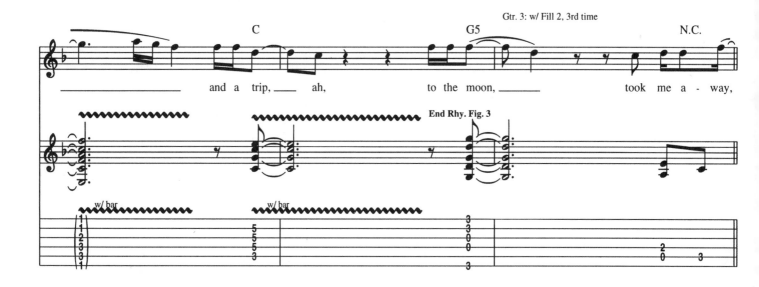

and a trip, _ ah, to the moon, _ took me a - way,

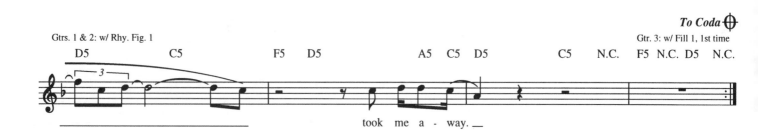

took me a - way. _

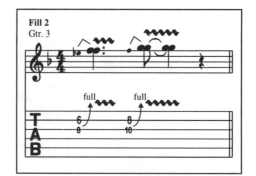

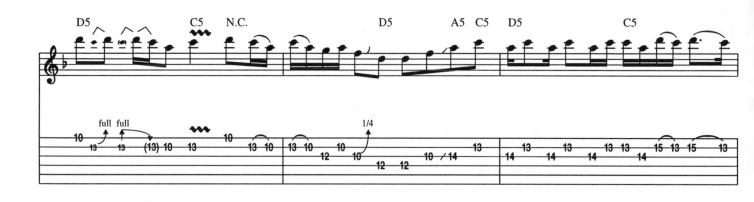

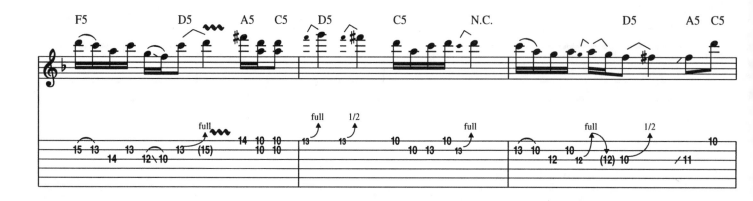

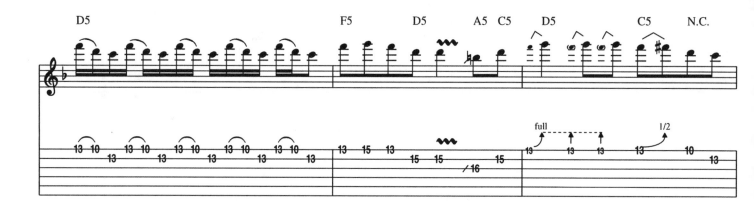

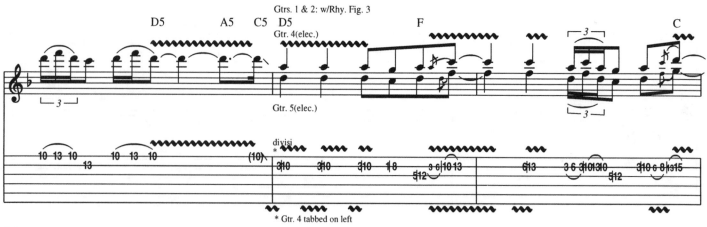

* Gtr. 4 tabbed on left

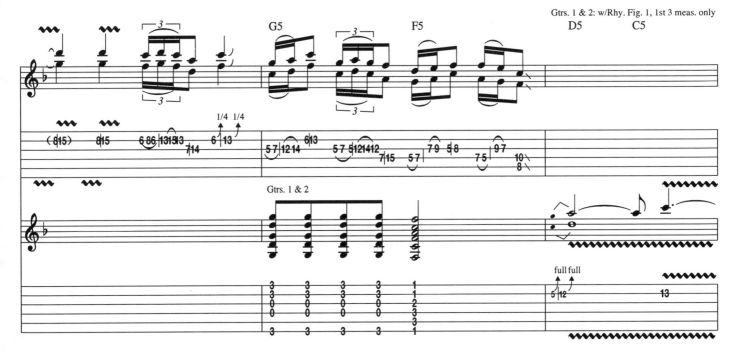

D.S. al Coda

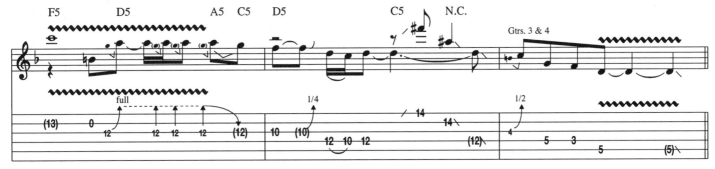

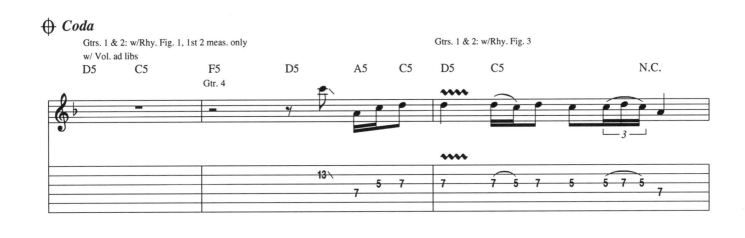

$\oplus$ *Coda*

Gtrs. 1 & 2: w/Rhy. Fig. 1, 1st 2 meas. only
w/ Vol. ad libs

Gtrs. 1 & 2: w/Rhy. Fig. 3

Gtrs. 1 & 2: w/ Rhy. Fig. 1, simile, till end

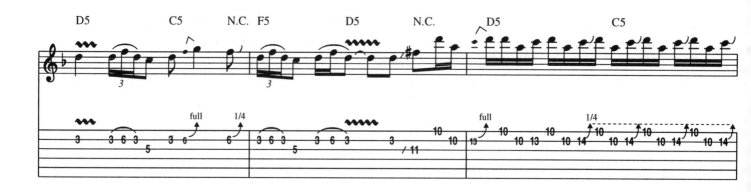

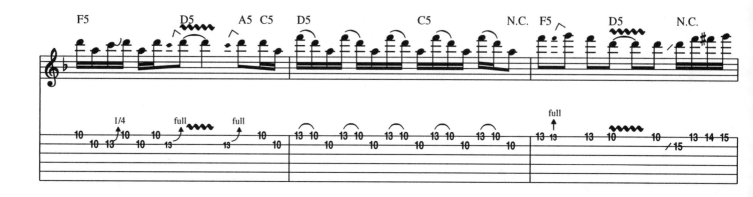

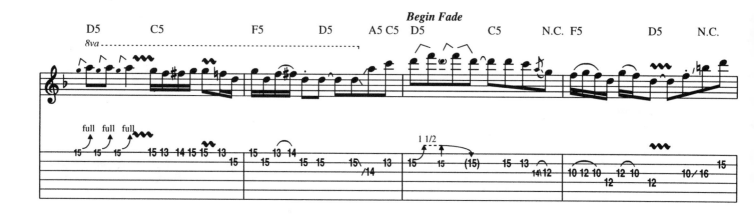

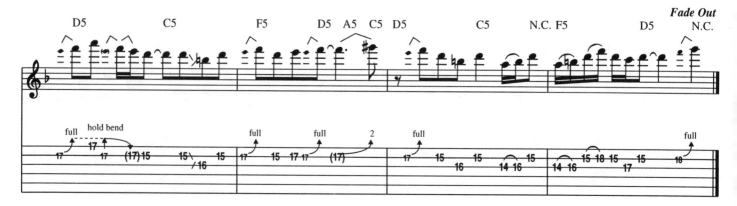

On The Hunt

Words and Music by Allen Collins and Ronnie Van Zant

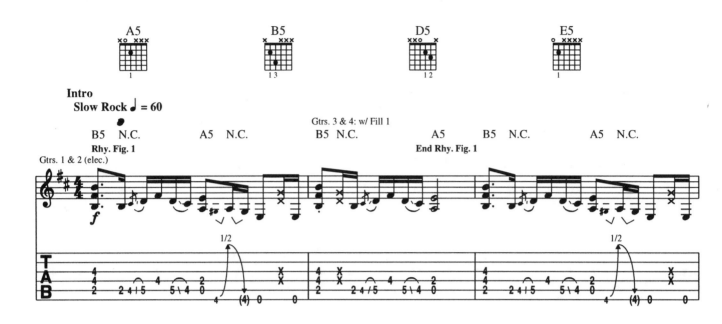

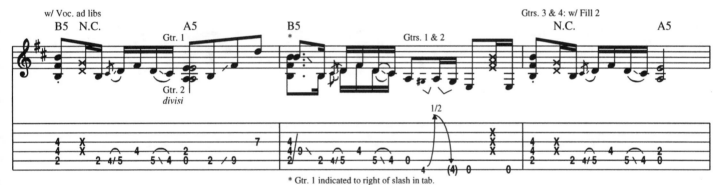

* Gtr. 1 indicated to right of slash in tab.

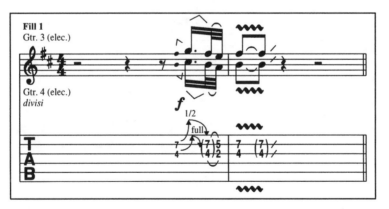

MCA music publishing

Saturday Night Special

Words and Music by Edward King and Ronnie Van Zant

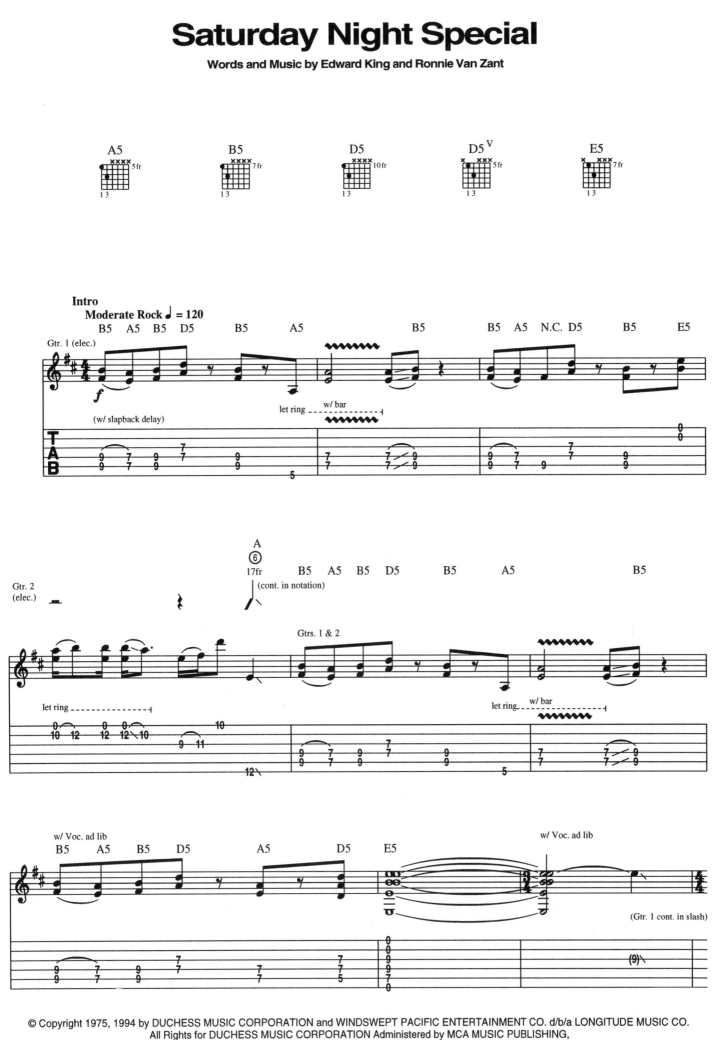

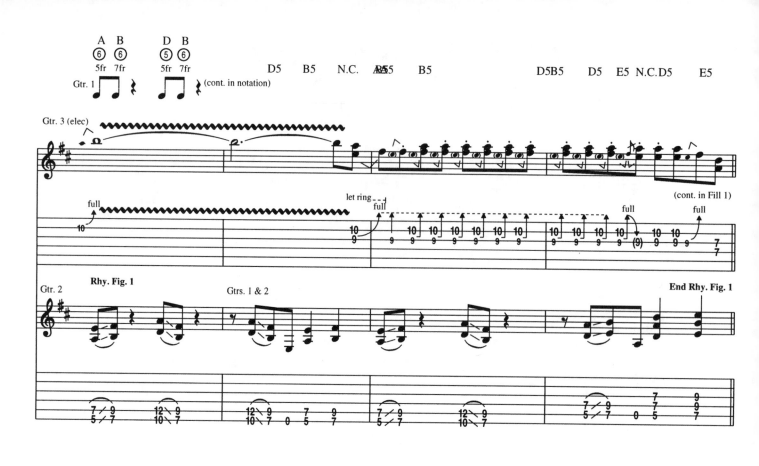

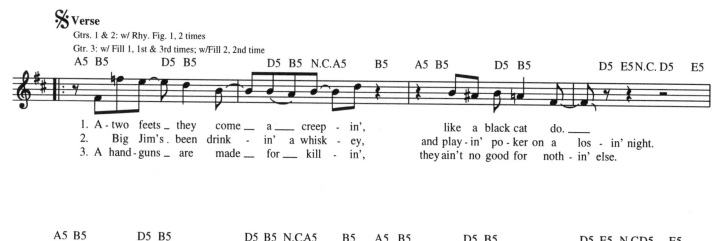

%% Verse

Gtrs. 1 & 2: w/ Rhy. Fig. 1, 2 times
Gtr. 3: w/Fill 1, 1st & 3rd times; w/Fill 2, 2nd time

1. A - two feets _ they come _ a _ creep - in', like a black cat do. _
2. Big Jim's _ been drink - in' a whisk - ey, and play - in' po - ker on a los - in' night.
3. A hand - guns _ are made _ for _ kill - in', they ain't no good for noth - in' else.

And two bod - ies are lay - in' a na - ked, a creep - er think he got a - noth - in' to lose. _
And pret - ty soon ol' Jim starts a think - in', a some - bod - y been cheat - in' and a ly - in'. _
And if you like to drink _ ol' whisk - ey, you might e - ven a shoot your - self. _

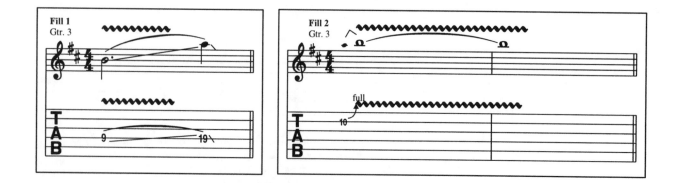

Spe - cial, ___ got a bar - rel that's a blue and cold. ___

To Coda ⊕

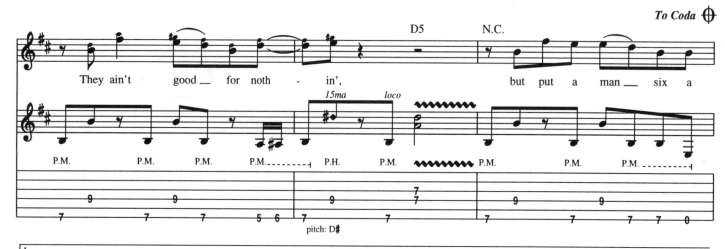

They ain't good ___ for noth - in', but put a man ___ six a

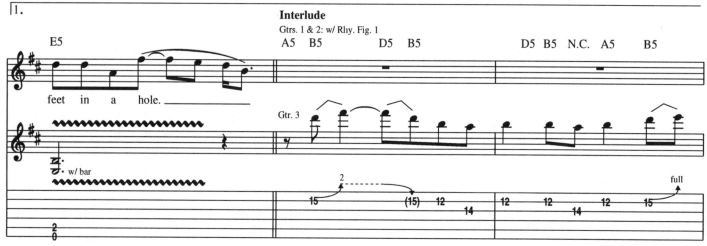

Interlude
Gtrs. 1 & 2: w/ Rhy. Fig. 1

feet in a hole. ___

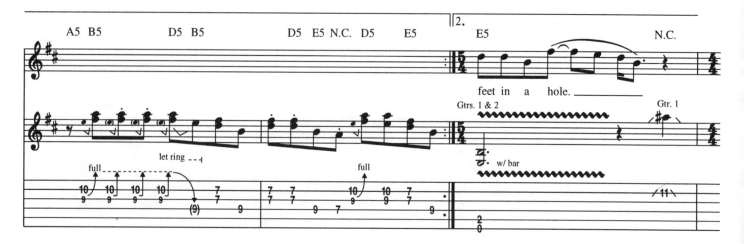

feet in a hole. ___

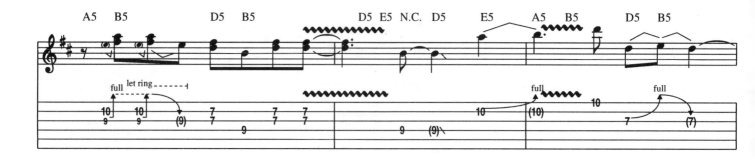

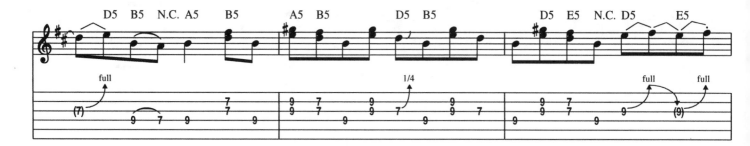

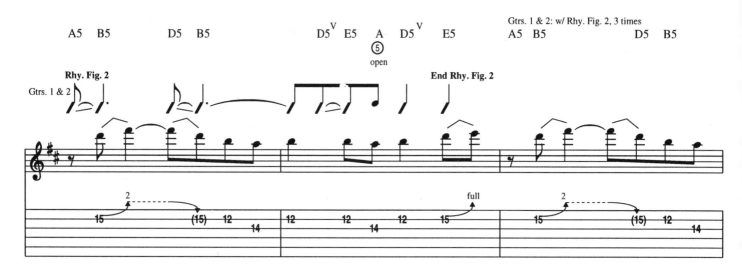

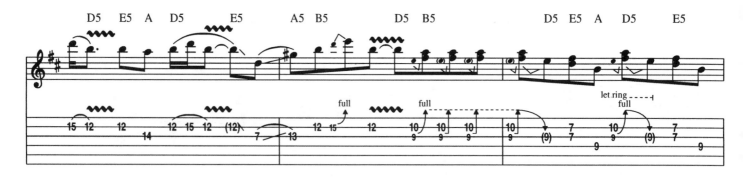

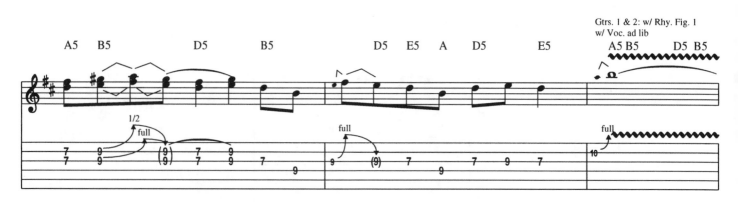

Simple Man

Words and Music by Ronnie Van Zant and Gary Rossington

MCA music publishing

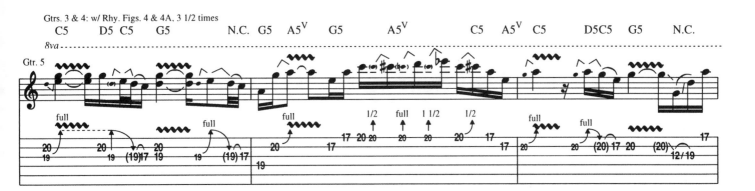

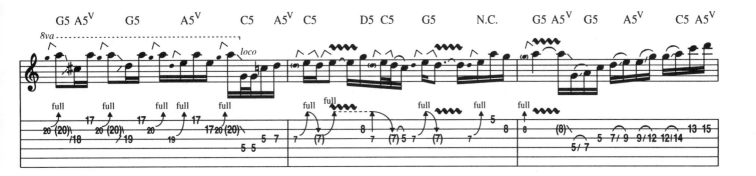

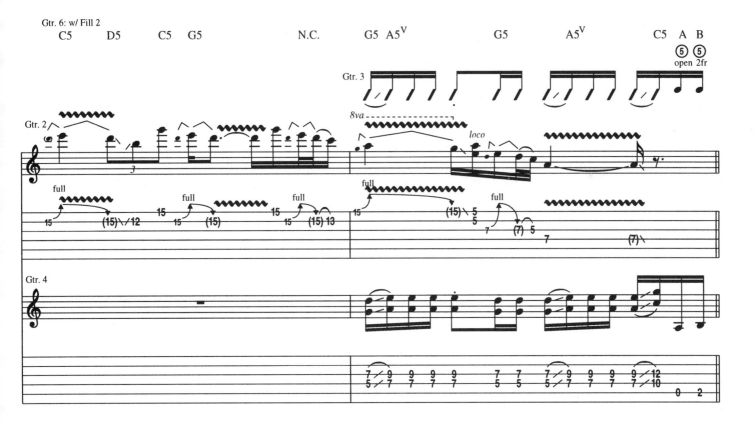

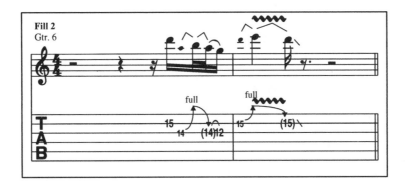

Gtrs. 1 & 2: w/ Rhy. Figs. 1 & 2, 2 times
Gtrs. 3 & 4: w/ Riff A

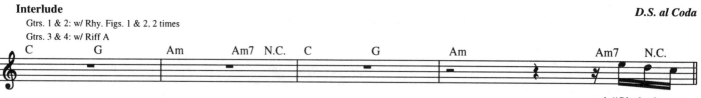

4. "Oh don't you

Additional Lyrics

3. "Forget your lust for the rich man's gold,
   All that you need is in your soul.
   And you can do this if you try.
   All that I want for you my son
   Is to be satisfied."

4. "Oh don't you worry, you'll find yourself.
   Follow your heart, and nothin' else.
   And you can do this if you try.
   All that I want for you my son
   Is to be satisfied."

Sweet Home Alabama

Words and Music by Ronnie Van Zant, Ed King and Gary Rossington

MCA music publishing

*Depress and release trem. bar at each beat indicated

Verse

Gtr. 1: w/ Rhy. Fig. 1
Gtr. 2: w/ Riff A, 1 3/4 times

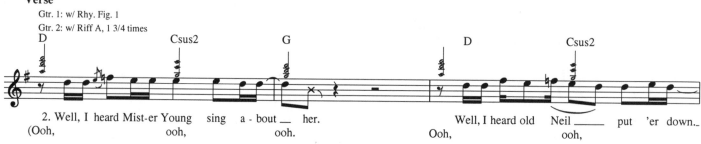

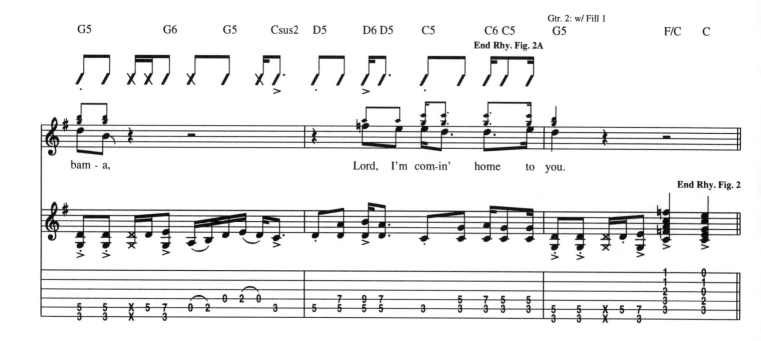

bam - a, Lord, I'm com-in' home to you.

Guitar Solo

Gtr. 1: w/ Rhy. Fig. 3, 2 times

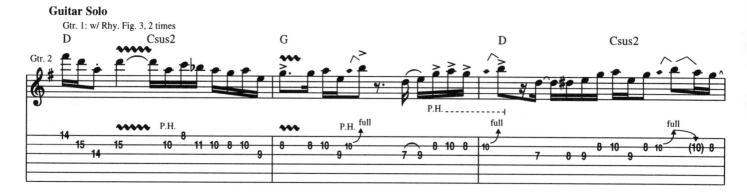

Verse

Gtr. 2: w/ Riff A, 1st meas. only

Gtr. 2: w/ Riff C (see p. ?)

3. In Bir-ming-ham they love the gov - 'nor, boo, boo,

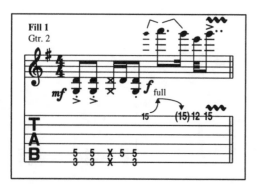

Guitar Solo

Gtr. 1: w/ Rhy. Fig. 4

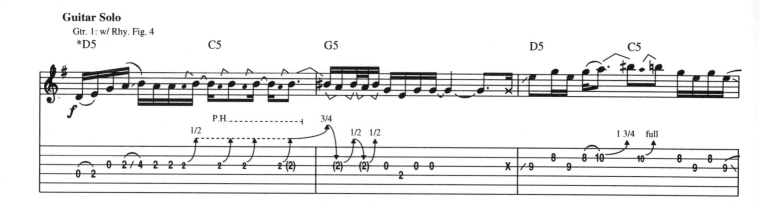

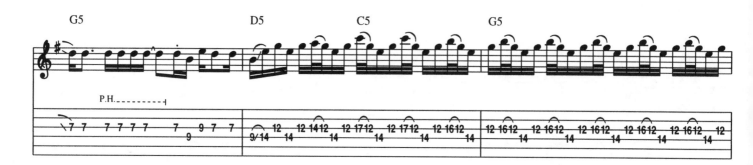

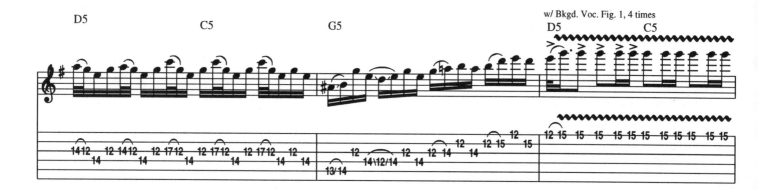

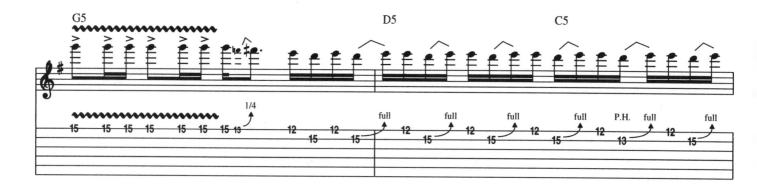

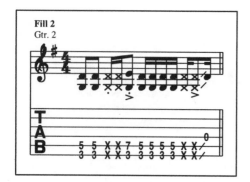

Fill 2

Gtr. 2

Ah,   ah,   ah,   Al-a-bam-a!

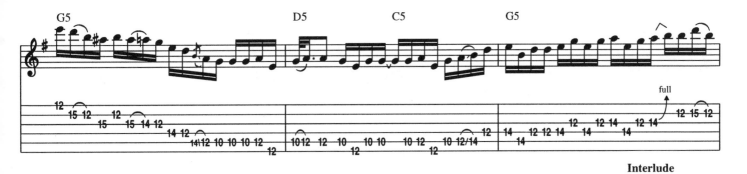

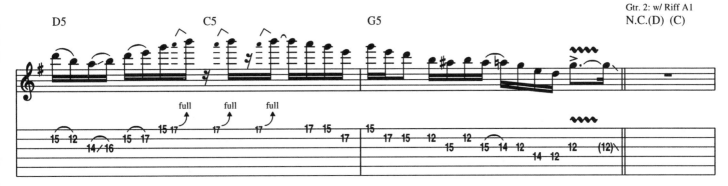

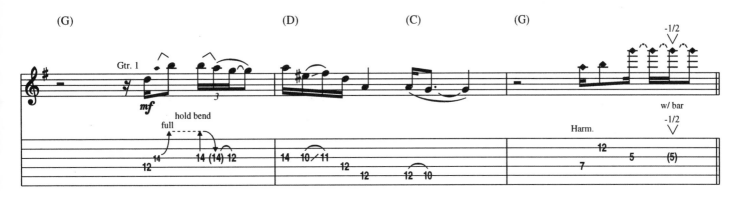

Verse
Gtr. 1: w/ Rhy. Fig. 1
Gtr. 2: w/ Riff A, 2 times

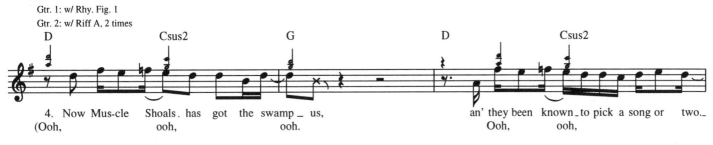

4. Now Mus-cle Shoals. has got the swamp __ us, an' they been known __ to pick a song or two. __
(Ooh, ooh, ooh. Ooh, ooh,

ooh, yes they do! __ Lord they get me off __ so __ much,
Ooh, ooh, ooh,

Chorus
Gtr. 1: w/ Riff B1   Gtr. 1: w/ Rhy. Fig. 2
Gtr. 2: w/ Riff B   Gtr. 2: w/ Rhy. Fig. 2A

they pick me up __ when I'm feel-in' blue __ 'n' now how 'bout you?   Sweet __ home Al - a -
pick me up __ when I'm feel-in' blue. __)

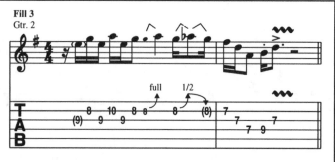

Tuesday's Gone

Words and Music by Allen Collins and Ronnie Van Zant

MCA music publishing

96

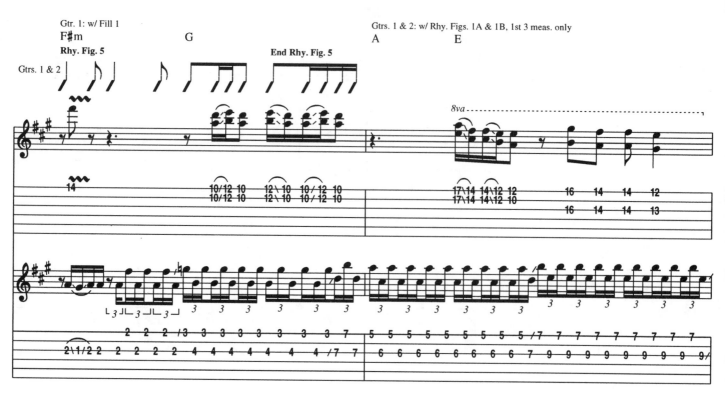

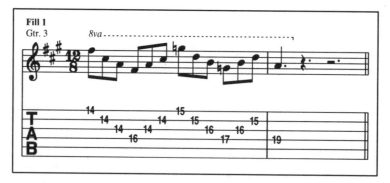

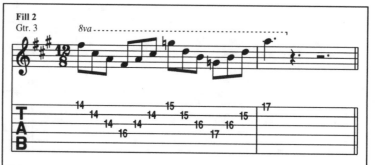

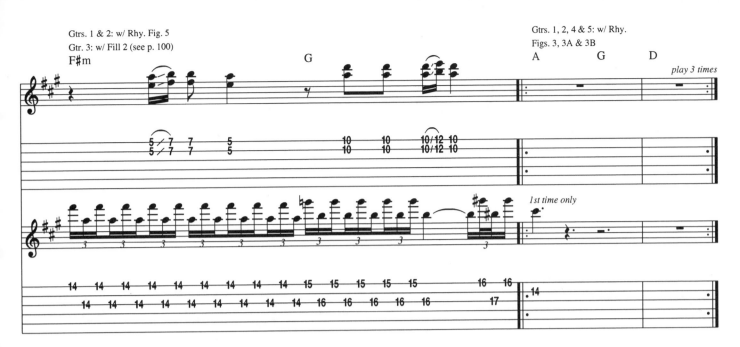

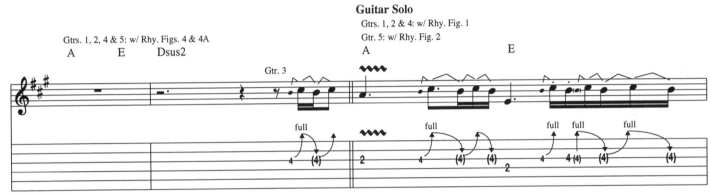

Guitar Solo

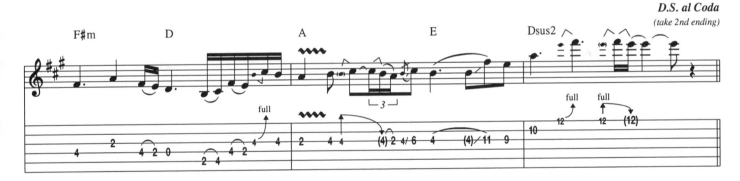

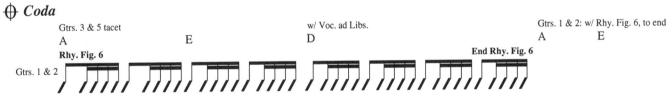

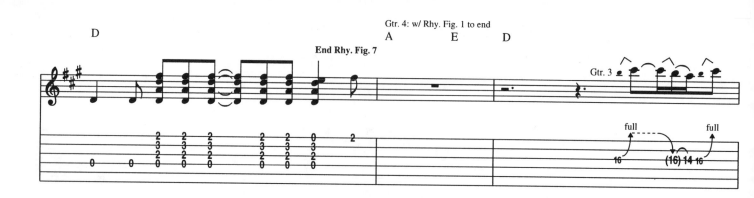

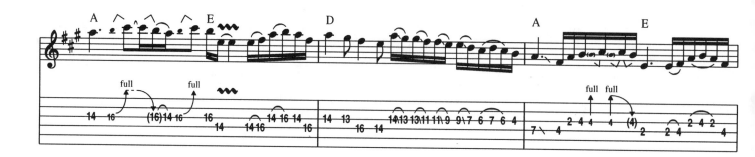

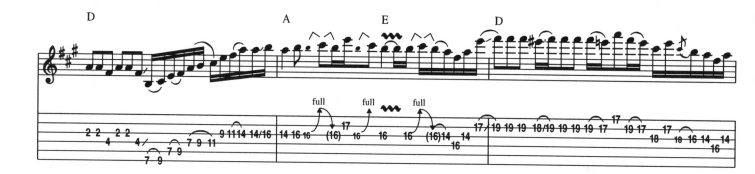

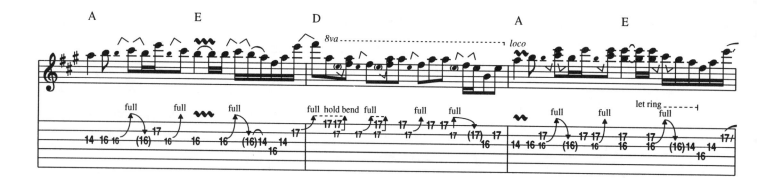

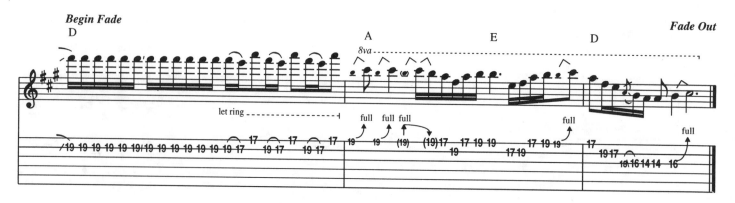

What's Your Name

Words and Music by Gary Rossington and Ronnie Van Zant

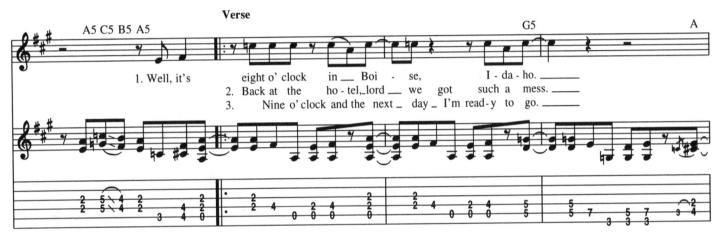

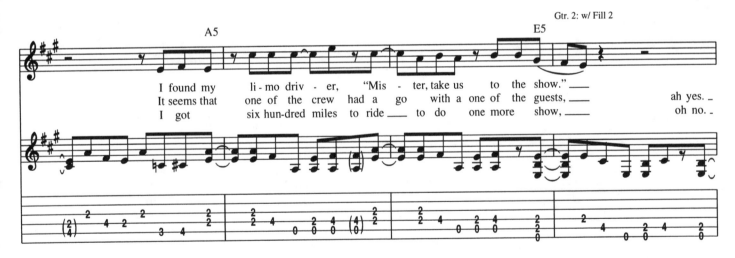

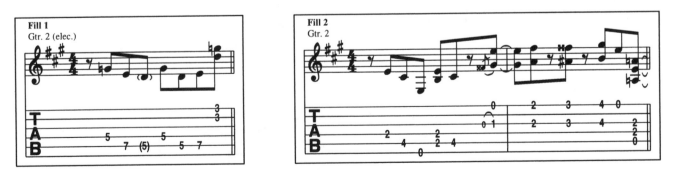

Fill 4
* Gtr. 2

* Horns arr. for gtr.

Fill 6
* Gtr. 2

* Piano arr. for gtr.

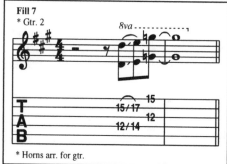

Fill 7

* Gtr. 2

* Horns arr. for gtr.

D.S. al Coda
(take 1st ending)

What's your name,

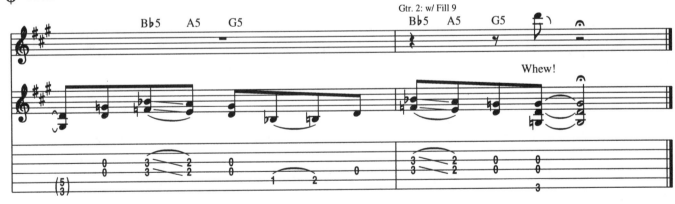

Gtr. 2: w/ Fill 9

Whew!

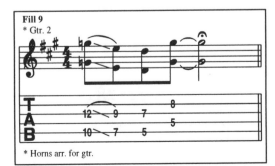

Fill 9
* Gtr. 2

* Horns arr. for gtr.

Whiskey Rock-A-Roller

Words and Music by Edward King, Ronnie Van Zant, and Billie Powell

* Includes subsequent parts in slashes by Gtr. 2.

MCA music publishing

I hope the peo-ple are __ read-y there, __ 'cause the boys are all __ read-y to go. __
The on-ly time __ I'm __ sat-is-fied __ is when I'm __ a on the road. __
And ev'-ry time __ I see __ that gal, Lord, __ she wants to take me down. __

Chorus

Well, I'm a whis-key a rock-a __ rol-ler, that's what I am. __

Gtrs. 1 & 3
* Rhy. Fig. 2

* Includes Gtr. 2.

Wo-men, whis-key, and miles __ of trav'-lin', it's all I __ un-der-stand. __

Gtrs. 1, 2 & 3   End Rhy. Fig. 2

Gtrs. 1, 2, & 3: w/ Rhy. Fig. 1, 1st 4 meas. only

Fill 1
Gtr. 4